ALL FUN BUT NO GAMES

BY: SHAWDAE

Shawdae

All Fun But No Games

ISBN: TBD

Dedication

I want to give a special thanks to my big sis, Ewina Harris.

The love and support you give are very much appreciated.

Thank you, Chasity Dunlap, for being there for me. I will

always cherish our friendship! Chinara Kendrick, thank you

for your love and support, I enjoyed being part of your video

shoot! Smooches.

Shawdae

Chapter 1

Man, do I need a fucking vacation! I swear, I am being pulled in every single direction of my life and can't seem to catch my breath for five minutes. My son will be having surgery soon, so I've been stressed about that, along with everything else. Bills, schooling, the kids; the weight of it all falls on me and I can't seem to catch a damn break these days. I swear, if I don't get a break soon, I'm going to lose my shit.

The universe must have heard me because as soon as I pulled into the Marathon gas station, my phone rang. It was Keyonna; one of my close friends for the past seven years. I picked up.

"Hey, boo," she said. "What you doing?"

"Shit! Stressed the fuck as usual. Why? What's up?"

"Well, hopefully this will cheer you up. You got some money?"

I was thinking, *She's about to ask me for some money. I mean, I know she can hold her own, but if she needs something and I have it, she got it, too.*

"I got called to do a video shoot in L.A. You wanna go with me and make some money?"

"HELL YEA! Let me make some calls to see if I can get a sitter for the kids. Ima hit you back in a few to get the details."

"Bet! Let me know, girl, and we outta here!"

I hung up and called every number I could in my phone. My usual sitter wanted more than usual to keep them all for more than three days.

I said to myself, *Damn, if you want ya rent paid for the month, just say that.*

She was way outta pocket with the number she threw at me. I called my backup and she said she wouldn't be available. My excitement quickly turned to disappointment because I was having trouble trying to secure a sitter. I had to call Keyonna back and let her know I wouldn't be able to make the trip. I mean, it was last minute, so I knew it was a stretch to get someone to keep them. I called her back.

"I'm not going to be able to go. My sitter's doing the most, trying to charge me an arm and a leg for a couple days out of town."

"Hold up, girl. Let me make a quick call to my cousin, Trina. She babysits for a living, so I'm sure she won't mind making some extra cash and won't charge you much. In the meantime, just get ya shit together so we can catch this flight."

I knew of her cousin but didn't know her personally. I knew she wouldn't have me taking my kids to someone who was going to put them in harm's way. I started to get excited again. I started twerking in the car and thinking I had to get myself some new shit for the trip. I had four days to get ready and wanted to do a little shopping before then. I decided since I had a little more time on my hands, I would take a trip over to Nordstrom's.

As soon as I hit the store, my phone started vibrating. I looked down at the message. It was Key. "GIRL PACK YO SHIT!"

I guessed she was able to get her cousin to watch the kids for me. I was souped as hell walking in the mall. I was ready to shop and get away from the madness of life for a few days. I thought about everything I needed to do over the next couple of days. Getting myself and the kids together; I had to make sure they were also straight; couldn't just think about myself. I made a list of everything I needed to do. So much to take care of but in so little time.

It was the day before the trip and Keyonna and I decided to go to the nail salon to get our nails done. She was going on and on about everything she wanted to do when we got there, all the places she wanted to see and, of course, the video shoot. You could tell she was just as excited as me, but it was something she was used to doing anyway.

Keyonna was no stranger to video shoots; she did them all the time in Atlanta. She'd done a few in Miami and maybe one or two in L.A. She was your typical, well-maintained video vixen. Nice body, hair always done, a Louis Vuitton bag for every occasion.

I mean, I'd done a few shoots here and there, but not like her since I had my kids to think about. She could up and go anytime she wanted since she had none, but me; I had to turn them down every now and then because I couldn't just up and travel and leave my kids at the last minute.

My son, Deon, required a lot of care. Hence, the reason for his surgery, so I couldn't leave him with just any and everybody. It would've been nice if I could've left him with his dad, but he was not reliable either.

Trina was a certified babysitter and Keyonna told me she even worked with kids that required a little extra care, so that was a relief to know he would be in great hands while I was gone.

It was the morning of; the kids and I were all packed and ready to go. I loaded them all in the car, along with all the bags. As I headed over to Trina's house, I gave them all the talk about being on their best behavior and looking out for one another.

We got to her house and I hurried up to unpack all their stuff from the car. Gave them all hugs and kisses before standing outside and giving her instructions and contact numbers for me and my emergency contacts. I slid her the money she asked for, along with an extra $200 on top of it.

She looked at me as if to say, "This is too much."

I gave her a hug and a smile and thanked her before jumping back in my truck and hitting I-285. Our flight was at 10:15 a.m. so we had to make sure we were at the airport at a reasonable time.

I got to Keyonna's house and saw her standing outside with her shades, a hoodie and jeans on, with her bags laid out on the hood of her car. She told me to park my truck in the garage while we waited for her friend, Jordan, to pick us up and take us to the airport. I was nervous to leave my kids but elated to be going on a much-needed trip.

Jordan pulled up blasting C-Breezy's "Go Crazy" on the radio. We hopped in the car and pulled off. I started dancing in my seat because it had hit me that, for the next couple of days, I wouldn't have to listen to my kids screaming and crying and I didn't have to worry about changing diapers. I could relax a little, have a couple shots, and let my hair down a bit.

We reached the Atlanta Hartsfield-Jackson International Airport just in time to check our bags and walk down to TSA. They were on some bullshit though, making me stand to the side to recheck my carry-on bag. I really didn't think nothing of it until their asses threw away all my damn body wash.

I said, "You know what? I don't have time for this, so yeah, throw it all away. I need to catch my flight."

I rolled my eyes and put my hand on my hips and shook my damn head and got the hell on. We'd overpacked our carry-ons, so we were walking slow as hell, but we made it to the gate with forty-five minutes to spare.

It was still early, so not too many food spots were open in the airport. We were both hungry as hell and decided to get some food from one of the breakfast spots. We asked this guy that was sitting next to us to watch our bags. He looked like he was on the up and up and wasn't going to run off with them. I mean, why would he? We were all on the same flight.

We left our seats and walked back up the ramp. Key was on her phone, going ham on her manager. He was on some snake shit, trying to get paid for an event she booked her damn self, but she checked his ass in 2.5 seconds on that one.

As we were waiting, her other line beeped. She said, "Damn, Charles, let me call you right back." She clicked over like, "Yeah what's up? Where you at?"

I didn't know who she was talking to, but hell, it didn't matter to me. I was just glad to be there with her. The clerk called both numbers out: 327 and 328.

I slid through the line like, "Oh yeah, that's us."

I grabbed my bag and passed Keyonna hers, grabbed a few ketchup packets and napkins, popped a straw in my cup, and headed back to our seats.

She was on the phone like, "Yeah, we on the way. We should be landing at the same time. We'll see u in a few hours." She whispered, "It's Andre, the one whose video I'm gonnna be in."

I was just like, "Oh, okay."

"He's on the plane now. Him, his cousin, and the girlfriend."

I said, "Well, everything good?"

She replied, "Yeah it's straight."

As the time passed, the whole time while I was eating, I was like, *God, please watch over us as we step foot on this plane. Let us make it there safe and back.*

Y'all know the silent prayer we all do before we board a flight. I had to laugh at myself a little, like I know I'm not scared but still let me just make sure God got my message.

All the passengers started to line up. I pulled out my boarding pass and got in line. We boarded the plane, and I went right for the window seat. The views from the sky are the best. As soon as I sat down, I turned my phone on to check any messages and to see what everybody else was doing on Instagram and FB. I was ready to pop my shit about the trip I was getting ready to take. I heard the flight attendant speaking, giving the directions and instructions as usual. Before you knew it, we were ready for take-off. West coast, here we come!!!

Chapter 2

My neck was cramped as hell after waking up from that long-ass flight. I was ready to get up and stretch my legs; we grabbed our carry-ons and waited to exit the plane to head down to baggage claim. We were waiting to meet up with Andre and his cousin. Andre was the rapper that asked Keyonna to do the shoot. He was established, already had three hit songs on the radio; but don't get me to lying as to what they were. He had enough money tho;enough to take care of all our needs while we were out here for the next few days.

We realized that there may have been an issue with the bags after waiting for almost thirty minutes for them to come down the belt. I decided to go over to the desk to ask if there was a problem with some of the bags because we had been waiting for quite some time for them to come around. The desk attendant informed us that there were some bags that came on an earlier flight and they were in a separate holding area upstairs.

Andre was mad as hell. "Damn, they couldn't make that announcement sooner to let us know? Da fuck."

We finally got the bags and headed outside to wait for our ride. Andre's manager arranged for us to travel in this nice-ass limo, fully stocked. He told the driver our location and we hit the highway. I was enjoying the views while driving through the city, taking pictures and reminiscing about the last time I was here. I was a long way from home, but it felt good to get away for a while.

After driving for about forty minutes, we arrived at this beautiful mansion in Beverly Hills. I had to go to the bathroom so bad, but I wanted to explore the house. It had nine bedrooms, a pool out back, and a waterfall feature surrounding the pool. I mean, I knew we were going to be staying somewhere nice, but I didn't think it would be this nice. I mean, there was a fireplace outside and a fire pit near the patio. I was moving so fast, trying to take pictures of everything, but I had to go to the bathroom. I went inside to find one and Keyonna was inside yelling for me to come get my bags, since the driver left them all at the front door. I was opening and closing all kinds of doors, trying to find the bathroom.

After running down this long hall, trying to find a restroom, I finally got to the last door. I opened it and inside this room was the most beautiful bathroom I had ever seen. There was a glass walk-in shower with a small T.V. up over the showerhead. There was a toilet as well as a bidet. I was in such awe over how the bathroom looked that I almost forgot how bad I had to pee. I started doing the pee pee dance as I headed over to the toilet. I sat there emptying my bladder just admiring this room because my bathroom back at home looked absolutely nothing like this one. I washed my hands and headed back down towards the living room.

"Alesha!!" I heard Keyonna calling me.

"What, heffa!?"

"Come get ya damn bags!" she yelled.

We were sharing a room, at least that's how it was supposed to go. I was noticing that her and Andre were very cozy in the limo, so I figured she may end up in the room with him. I also notice that his cousin came with someone and there was another couple as well on the trip. I thought for a minute that this was some kind of group thing that no one told me about and I was beginning to feel like the third wheel.

I was dragging my bags up the stairs and down another hall, trying to find my room, when I ran smack into this 6'2, caramel-colored, thick brother. I looked up at him and he was staring down at me with the brightest smile and asked if I needed help with my bags. I couldn't speak seem like, I gave him a once over and took a mental picture. He had on some grey sweats, with a nice bulge in the front and a Gucci t-shirt on and some clean-ass Air Force Ones.

Keyonna slapped me out of my trance. "Girl, he asked if you needed some help."

I stuttered, "Uh, yea, yes…yes I do. I was trying to find my room."

All the room keys were colored coded to the door locks and in this big-ass place, it was like walking around a funhouse trying to find the room.

"I'll help you," he said. "Let me grab this bag for you. I'm Christian, Andre's brother. I came a day early, so I know my way around the place. I can take you to your room."

Here go Keyonna's ass, "So, which room is yours, Christian?" as she side-eyed me.

He just laughed as we approached our room. I flashed him a smile and he winked as he walked away. Shit, he was fine; I was wondering if he was here with somebody since everybody else was.

Once we all got settled and showered, Andre suggested we all go out to eat. It was late and the temperature had dropped, and I realized I didn't pack a jacket. I only packed a few things, mostly shoes, since we said we would shop for some stuff once we got out here. I put on the warmest thing I had in my bag, but I was still going to be cold.

We were standing outside waiting for the car to arrive and I started rubbing my arms to keep warm, Christian noticed and came to stand by me, but the cars were pulling up by then. There were twp cars. Two couples in each car, they said.

Keyonna grabbed Andre's hand and they went to the front car and I stood there looking at her all cuddled up with him.

Andre turned around and looked at Christian. "Y'all can ride in that car and just follow behind us."

I smirked to myself because now this was starting to feel like a set-up to me. Like both Andre and Keyonna knew that Christian and I would be the odd pair out that they could put together. I hopped in the back and slid all the way over to the window; the other couple sat across from us.

Christian said, "Why you so far away? Come closer. I can see you're cold."

At first, I was thinking "nah," but he was so laid back and cool about it, that I felt like what the hell since he was right. I was cold as shit.

I slid over and he wrapped his arm around me. God, he smelled good as hell and his body heat was just what I needed to warm up. He whispered, "You know this was a set-up, right?"

"I figured as much," I said back.

We pulled up to the restaurant and he got out and grabbed my hand to help me out the car as he held the door open. He was such a gentleman, and I was really feeling him at this point. We were waiting for the other cars to arrive, so he came up behind me and wrapped his arms around me to keep me warm in the meantime. The other cars pulled up finally and we were all escorted to our table. It was outdoor seating in the back of this fancy restaurant; even the way they had the menus set up on the table was different.

Even though there were heat lamps over our table, I was still kind of cold. I sat down next to Christian and scooted as close as I could to him. He put his arm around me and whispered to me to order anything I wanted. I kept it cute and classy and got the salmon with rice and spinach,

We all sat around laughing, drinking and talking about the video shoot. The bill came and the guys at the table chipped in on the bill and Christian put in the most because he paid the tip as well. We all hopped in the cars and headed back to the mansion.

Keyonna decided to go sleep in the room with Andre, so because Christian and I were having such great conversation in the car, he asked if it was okay if he came to my room for the night. I said sure; I didn't have any expectations of anything but if anything did happen, I was okay with it.

Soon as we got back to the house, I went straight to my room and went straight for the shower. I was full and sleepy and wanted to take a nice hot shower and put on something warm and climb into bed.

I heard Christian come into the room while I was in the shower but didn't think anything of it. I didn't expect him to come into the shower with me. Although, standing there under the hot water got me to thinking about him putting his arms around me at the restaurant. He smelled so good, and his body was so warm. I came out here to support my friend on this shoot and to think I may have met a man in the process made me smile a bit.

I was under a lot of stress at home so Christian was like a breath of fresh air to me. I turned the water off and got dressed. As soon as I opened the bathroom door, I saw him sitting on the side of the bed with no shirt on and a towel in his hands.

"I was waiting for you to come out of the shower, so that I could go in, if that's okay?"

"Sure, it is. Go ahead and get yourself ready for bed."

I watched him walk into the bathroom and close the door. Part of me wanted to peek in while he was in there, so I could see what he was really working with, but I talked myself out of it.

I crawled into bed and waited for him to come out. I could barely keep my eyes open as I started dosing off. I perked up when I heard the shower turn off. I was nervous for him to come to bed with me, but also felt a sense of comfort because I just knew he wouldn't do anything to me that I didn't want him to do.

He could tell I was a bit uneasy, so he asked, "You good?"

"Yea," I said. I gave him the side eye. "Don't try no shit."

He laughed. "No worries. I'll be the perfect gentleman. I just figured since we were having such great conversation, that we could continue."

I said, "That's fine. Just know, if you try anything, you gonna wake up with a knot on your head."

"No pressure, sweetheart. I got you," he said as we both laughed.

We laid back and started talking about our plans for tomorrow and asking each other questions, getting to know one another. Eventually, I curled up in his arms and before you know it, we both were dozing off. I felt so at peace and protected being in his arms. If he did try anything, I would not have stopped him. I would've welcomed it with open arms and open legs.

Chapter 3

The next morning, I woke up and rolled over to find that Christian wasn't there. I sat up in the bed to see if he was in the bathroom and he wasn't. I got up, turned on the T.V. to the music station, and started looking for something to wear that day.

As I was in the bathroom washing my face, I heard a knock on the door. I told whoever it was to come in and it was him. He said he heard the music, so he came up to see what I was up to.

"You were sleeping to good, so I didn't want to wake you. Oh, yea, and you were snoring pretty loud, too," he said with a chuckle.

"Yea, right," I said.

"Listen, when you're done getting dressed, come downstairs so we can all go over what we are doing today."

I said, "Okay, cool. Be down in about twenty minutes."

I threw my clothes on and headed downstairs to the living room. There was Keyonna, on her phone taking selfies in the corner. Christian was on the phone, talking some sort of business while he was rolling up, and Andre was sitting by the bar smoking.

"Let's go check out this new food spot," Andre yelled out.

They called for the cars to come pick us all up for our outing. The weather was beautiful; the sun was shining bright, and there was a nice, mild breeze in the air. I sat back and took it all in. In another day or so, I would be heading back to my reality in Atlanta.

We pulled up to the restaurant and, again, we were given the VIP treatment. I have to say that Andre really made sure we all had the best while we were out here. I looked at the menu and decided I wanted caviar and a glass of red wine.

Here go Keyonna, saying, "That's that weird shit right there. Why you even ordering that nasty shit?"

I ignored her comment while I was laughing at something Christian was whispering in my ear. Andre started talking about the video shoot later that day.

"Okay, so this the move. At three, we will head over to the studio and do a little scene there. Then, later tonight, I have a T.V. show to do with one of the biggest networks, so we can all hang out until the filming takes place. That cool with ya'll?"

"Cool with me," I said.

Everyone else agreed. I grabbed Keyonna and pulled her outside near the back of the restaurant to take some pictures. I wanted to try to capture as much of these moments as I could and make memories for us because who knew when the next time would be that I'd be able to get away like that.

Once we got back to the table, Christian was finishing up and we noticed that his cousin had got up and left his girl at the table. They had been arguing since we got here, seemed like. Just over dumb shit. I mean, we were getting treated to the life of luxury and they were out here arguing and fussing over a bunch of bullshit.

We all grabbed our things and headed back to the house to change clothes for the show Andre had to do. We were in and out in under an hour. The drivers needed to hit the gas station, so while we were waiting for the drivers to pump the gas, Christian asked if I wanted anything out of the store. I told him no, but I loved how he always made sure to ask me if I wanted or needed anything. He ran inside to get some Backwoods so they could roll up in the car on the way to the station.

Traffic wasn't bad today, so we were able to make it there in about twenty minutes and we headed right in and up to the 17th floor. Andre had to head straight to set, but we were all able to watch on the screen from outside the studio. We had been up early and out most of the day, so I was getting sleepy standing here. I wanted to go back to the house and take a quick nap, but I knew there was more they had planned for the remainder of the day.

I decided to step out onto the balcony for some air. Christian came out five minutes after me and walked up to stand behind me.

He asked, "You okay?"

It was starting to feel like we were a couple, sorta. Whenever I moved, he moved right behind me to make sure I was good. I told him I was tired and needed to rest, I knew they wanted to hit up a club after this, but I didn't have the energy.

"If you tired, baby, let's just go back to the house. I'll tell Andre you aren't feeling good, and we can go back so you can get you some rest. You don't HAVE to do everything everyone else is doing."

I thought about it for a few, I really didn't want to leave Keyonna, but she was so wrapped up in everything Andre was doing, I didn't even think she would've cared too much if I decided to leave. "Let me let Keyonna know, and we can be out."

"Cool," he said.

I told Keyonna that I would see her back at the house. She shot me a side eye and said, "Okay."

We took one of the cars back to the house. As soon as we got inside, I needed a hot shower. I went to my room and took off my clothes and jumped in the shower. I stood under the hot water and let it soothe my body. I wasn't sure what Christian was doing, but a piece of me wished he had come in and got in the shower with me.

After I got out, I threw on a t-shirt and climbed into the bed to watch T.V. I started to dose off but, a few minutes later, I heard a soft knock on the door.

"Do you mind if I come in?" Christian asked.

"Nah, not at all."

He sat on the foot of the bed and started rolling up. "You smoking?" he asked.

"Sure, just pass it to me when you done."

Even though we talked a lot during that first night, he still wanted to know more about me. I told him that I was originally from Baltimore but that I lived in Atlanta with my kids. That I did movies, a few videos here and there, and I also did nails on the side.

"Damn, girl, you do a little bit of everything."

"I have kids I need to take care of, and I can't do that sitting on my ass," I told him.

He told me that he was also from the Atlanta area and basically wanted to know if we would hook up once we got back to town and back to regular everyday life. I had to make it clear to him that my kids came first and anytime I had that's for myself, I wouldn't mind spending it with him. We hadn't even passed the blunt back and forth that many times and I was high already. I guess, mainly because I was so tired from the day.

He continued the conversation by telling me that he wanted to come out with his own weed plant. That he was really interested in the Cannabis business and realized that there was money to be made there. He was a hustler like myself; I liked that shit.

We sat there smoking and vibing like we knew each other from way back. It would've been a great time to jump on the man, but that moment wasn't even about sex. It was simply about getting to know him, and I was really feeling everything about him.

We were so lost in conversation, we didn't even hear everyone else come back to the house. Christian and I went downstairs. They had arrived with food and drinks and had the music playing, like the whole scene was something out of a video itself. I was enjoying every minute of our time there.

They started talking about the plans for the next day. Christian wanted to hit up an outlet mall before the video shoot. He was saying he wanted to get a new sweat suit and I cosigned, "Yea, me too!"

He looked over at me and said, "Well, let's get up and go early while they all still sleep."

I said, "Sure, I'm down."

We were all up until at least one in the morning, smoking, drinking, and laughing at a bunch of dumb, random shit; enjoying the vibe.

The next morning, Christian and I got up to get ready to run to the outlets. He called a car to come pick us up and drop us off. He said, "Let's go to the Nike store."

It was an exclusive place that had three levels to it. We walked in and he grabbed my hand and said, "Get whatever you want."

I wasn't sure if I heard him right. "Huh?" Like I mean, I heard him, but I had to hear him say it again. So, I asked, "What you gonnna wear?"

"My favorite color: green. Help me find a shirt."

We were both looking and we came across a few, so I started grabbing shirts and pants for myself.

He said, "You good? That's all you want?"

I said "yeah" because I wasn't trying to be greedy and snatch up everything in there, even though he told me to get anything I wanted.

He then told me to get some shoes and to pick whatever kind I wanted. I couldn't believe that man; I was in shock at how cool he was with telling me to get any and everything I wanted.

I picked up one pair, but it didn't match with anything I had, so Christian helped me pick some shoes out. We both got a matching pair and then he got him another pair.

He asked me again, "You sure you good? You can shop some more if you want."

Now, any other chick would've been like, "Oh, okay," but that's not me. Trust me when I tell you, there was plenty more I could've grabbed but I wasn't about to be like that. So, I said, "Yeah. Come on; let's get in line."

We walked up to the register and placed all of our clothes on the counter. As the man was ringing everything up, I said to myself, "DAMN!"

We were at $1500 and he was still ringing stuff up. Our total came to $2300, and Christian wasn't fazed by it one bit.

He actually couldn't believe that it was so cheap. "That's it?!"

His ass didn't give a shit; money wasn't an issue to him, and he made that very clear. We grabbed our bags and headed back to the house.

Soon as we got back, the whole house was up. I dropped my bags in my room on the floor and went to check on Keyonna. "Damn, bitch! You just left me, but you the main one talking about we need to stick together."

I said, "Bitch, shut-up. Ya ass was sleep so don't act like I just left you here for good and left you here all day."

She followed me back to my room. "So, what all y'all get?"

I shrugged my shoulders. "Nothing much. Just some shoes and a couple of outfits from a few stores and the Nike outlet."

Then there came the cousin's girlfriend, Asia, walking in like, "Damn, okay. You don't even know him like that, and he's spending big bands on you, girl?"

I said, "Girl, it is what it is. I'm here for Keyonna ass tho."

"You like him tho, don't you?"

I looked at her. "Hmm...maybe."

"Ain't no maybe, bitch. You two been up under each other the whole time since y'all met."

I rolled my eyes. "Honey, you all in my business. Don't do that. This shit doesn't excite me. I can get my own money, but it was nice of him to do for me."

They both looked at me.

"Did you fuck him?" Keyonna asked.

I said, "Nah, and he hasn't tried anything with me either, so we good." I turned them around, pushing them towards the door. "Bye! Get out! Get out!"

They were being messy, so they had to go.

Chapter 4

While I waited on everyone else to get their shit together for us to go do the video shoot, I decided to give Trina a call to check on my kids. She wouldn't call me unless something was wrong, but I still needed to talk to my babies. She picked up on the second ring,

"Hey y'all! What y'all doing?"

They all started smiling and waving in the camera. "Hey, Mama! We miss you!"

"I miss y'all, too. Y'all being good for Ms. Trina?"

In unison, they yelled, "Yeah!"

Trina said, "Yeah, girl; they good. They in here watching a movie, eating popcorn and pizza. When the sun goes down, we will head over to the park so they can run around a bit."

"Okay, cool. Thank you so much again and if u need me, call me."

"Of course, you know I will. Enjoy the rest of your trip and I'll see you soon."

Soon as we hung up, I texted my sister, Ayanna.

> *Hey Sis. I'm good; just checking on you.*
>
> *Everything good?*
>
> *Hell yeah!*
>
> *Well, good. I need to make sure you good at all times. Now drop ya damn location!*

I laughed so hard,

> *Ok, I got you.*
>
> *I'm serious, do it now! Ok?*
>
> *Sis, I got you; doing it right now.*
>
> *You too far from home. Gotta make sure my lil sis straight.*

I had to make sure I let my sis know where I was exactly so she wouldn't worry. I dropped my location to her and by the time I was done with my calls, they were all ready to go to the shoot finally.

We had a long-ass ride to go the boat. The scene they were shooting was located in Long Beach and we needed to catch the sun while it was up. I had brought a swimsuit, but I wasn't wearing it. I didn't even get in the pool back at the house, so I wasn't really feeling getting in the pool on the boat.

We arrived at Long Beach, waiting on the cameraman to show up and for them to bring the boat to the dock. So, while they waited on all the equipment, I decided to start snapping pictures. I took a few by the palm trees, then Christian and I took a few. I swear, it felt like we were a couple, even though we weren't one. The conversations, the pictures, shopping and just being close. I was liking every bit of it and all the attention he was giving me made me feel good.

The boat was ready for us to board. They started popping Moët bottles and filling cups up. I grabbed me a cup and sat back and watched as they started shooting the video. I took a few pics and made a few videos to send Keyonna once she was done. You know, I was just trying to be the supportive friend.

While they were shooting, I had to check on my flight really quick to make sure my time was right for 4:15 p.m. I didn't wanna go back home yet, but I knew that reality was slowly approaching. I hadn't had a break that long in years and I was really trying to enjoy myself as much as I could. As soon as I got back to the A, I would be back to Mama duties and have to start preparing myself for my son's surgery.

Once they got done, we returned back to the side of the dock. I wanted to ride around and check the city out. We all wanted to, but everyone wanted to go somewhere different. So, we all decided to split up and go our own way. Keyonna and I figured we would go together, so she had Andre sent a private car for us.

First, we went to get food and then went out cruising the city. We took a ride up on Crenshaw to pay our respects to one of the greatest rappers that had recently been killed in front of his store: Nipsey.

When we pulled up, the entire block was lit with folks taking pictures and making videos. The line was long as hell but, eventually, we made our way to the front and took our pictures. Then we drove around a little more, catching the sights and soaking in the city. My phone began to vibrate; it was Christian.

"Hey, what's up? Where y'all at?"

I said, "Out enjoying the view."

He said, "Oh yeah? Oh okay... well, what time y'all going back to the house?"

I said, "Shortly. Why? What's up?"

"Well, I'm almost done where I'm at and just letting you know I'll be back at the house soon. So, I'll meet you there."

"Okay, cool. See you in a bit."

Keyonna was sitting there with this look on her face. "Are y'all friends or is he yo nigga? 'Cause, girl, he clocking you like you his girl or something."

I said, "Girl, damn, you nosey but anyway, let's head on back to the house so I can meet my man."

We both started laughing. I was ready to get back to him. I had slick caught some feelings for his young ass. Just off the way he had been treating me since I had gotten there; not what he had done for me. Just the feeling I got from him treating me the way I knew that I deserved to be treated by a man.

We got back to the house and all the lights were on. I was looking like, oh yeah, he beat us here, which was even better. I walked in, looking for his fine ass. He came out the kitchen like, "What's up, girl?"

He gave me a hug and kissed me on my forehead. I said to myself, *I don't know what's going on here, but I can damn sure get used to this. I would love to be up under him all the time.*

Later that night, we chilled and watched a movie up in my room again. It felt good laying on him, and he smelled so damn good. I was laying in his arms and he had them wrapped around me, holding me tight. His soft hands were rubbing on my booty. If he didn't stop, the booty rub was going to turn into me giving him some booty for real.

He fired up a blunt, but I didn't smoke that time. I sat up and scooted closer to him. I leaned in with my head to the side and kissed the side of his neck. He returned the favor and kissed the side of mine. He squeezed my nipple ring as he continued to kiss and lick the side of my neck. I was just waiting for him to slide his hands down my panties so he could see how wet he was making me. He put his blunt out, flipped me over, and pulled my shorts off.

He began to run his hands between my thighs until he got to the kitty. He slipped two fingers inside and looked me in my eyes. "I make you this wet, huh?" he whispered.

He put a condom on and started to deep stroke my pussy, pushing every bit of him inside of me. I felt all the stress and worry I had on my mind leave my body at that very moment. He gripped my waist nice and tight and applied all pressure to the pussy while he kissed me from the back of my neck to the crack of my ass. This wasn't just some regular fuck; he took his time to make love with each stroke he made. The slower and harder he stroked, the wetter and wetter my pussy got. His dick was so got-damn good, I started winding my hips on it.

My eyes began to roll in the back of my head as I let him take full control. I came all over his dick, I hadn't had sex in about eight months, so that right there was everything I needed and then some.

He nutted and collapsed onto me as we both lay on the bed. I tried to make my way to the bathroom, but I couldn't walk or stand up straight. My legs were so weak, I felt like he took my soul out of me and I needed a minute to sit until it came back.

I pulled myself together and walked into to the bathroom and ran the shower. A nice hot shower was perfect after that. I got in and stood there for a moment with a smile on my face because that nigga had really put it on me.

Just as I was about to pour the soap on my washcloth, Christian came in behind me. He took my washcloth from me and began to wash my back. He took his time and kissed everywhere before washing it. I could feel myself getting wet all over again. He reached his hand around me and started to rub my breasts as he continued to wash my back. I turned around to face him and that dick was standing straight up at attention, like he was ready for round two.

We took our time and washed each other up, while we slowly kissed and enjoyed each other's body. We stepped out and he wrapped me in a towel and wrapped one around his waist. We headed back to the bed where he told me to lay down and then we went for round two.

I was still trying to regain my energy from round one but his dick was so damn big and juicy, with those veins in it looking like a fat Snickers bar. He propped my leg up on top of his shoulder, held on tight to my waist, and thrusted himself inside me again.

I let him fuck my pussy any which way he wanted to. I was moaning and he started talking me through my next nut, saying all kinds of freaky shit. "Cum on Daddy's dick for me."

He started telling me how good my pussy was and how he wanted to take the condom off. He didn't though and as he stroked my pussy some more, I began to let out a deep sigh. That surge of cum I released felt like a warm waterfall. He nutted again and kissed me softly on the lips as he pulled out.

We cleaned up again and I threw on a t-shirt and spread out across the bed. That dick was so damn good, it had me sleeping like a newborn baby. I thought he was going to go back to his room, but he snuggled up next to me and fell right to sleep. Moments like that, I could definitely get used to.

The next morning, we decided to do a little more shopping before leaving the following day. The first stop was the edible store. I walked in with my mind set to buy only two packs of gummies, but all that changed when I walked in. They had so many different kinds to choose from. I decided to buy four different packs and Christian bought a few for the both of us. We went edible crazy; it was like being a kid in the candy store. I told Keyonna we had to try the raspberry box, but we would have to eat first. We needed to have a full stomach after our purchase.

We all drove to Roscoe's House of Chicken N' Waffles and sat outside at the tables while we waited on our food to get done. I sat there with the biggest smile on my face, thinking about the night before, but no one noticed. Until I looked up and saw Christian looking me right in my face. I smiled at him and he smiled back. With a smirk on my face, I asked what he was looking at. He replied, "Nothing," and he laughed to himself and held his head down.

He knew where my mind was at that moment and we both tried to play it cool. He got up from the table to go get our food and when he came back, we started eating and discussing things about the edibles. He kept asking me would I give him one of mine. I said that we could take one together when we got back to the house after we got done hanging out for the day.

After we ate, we went to the studio rooftop to meet up with some friends of Andre's. I was enjoying the view of the city; standing there looking at the sky reminded me of the time when I used to live in Cali. I loved it, but the lifestyle every day was something that became too much for me.

Our vacation was coming to an end. We only had a day and a half left so I had to make sure I made the best of it. My reality back home was starting to kick in, like damn; but like they say, all good things come to an end, but this ending wasn't a bad one. Not in any way. I couldn't have asked for a better vacation.

Shawdae

Chapter 5

Early the next morning, Keyonna and I decided to take a walk around the block. We were leaving tomorrow and wanted to get out and enjoy our last day in Cali. We decided that we would take our edibles while we were on our stroll. She ate hers first; then I ate mine. We knew we had about a good hour before they kicked in, so we decided to keep on walking and figured by the time we headed back to the house, it would be kicking in good. We found a bench near a small park that we sat down on and had some much-needed girl talk.

We were talking about our baby daddies and the kids and what not when suddenly, I felt a fast rush of calm shoot through my body.

I stared at Keyonna and she looked at me like, "Bitch, what's wrong with you?"

I replied, "I think I'm high. Like high... high."

"Stop playing, Alesha; we still got a little while before they kick in. So, stop."

Not within five minutes of her saying that, she stopped talking and got super quiet as she sat there staring into space. She turned really slow towards me with a confused look on her face and asked, "You hear that?" We sat there looking at each other, confused as fuck. "You don't hear that man calling you?"

"Bitch, you are tripping. Ain't nobody calling me."

However, I wasn't sure if she was telling the truth or not, so I started looking around to see if anyone was there. I sat there and started laughing to myself. Keyonna put her head down and closed her eyes but then suddenly jumped up in a panic. I just looked at her because I wasn't too sure what was happening. I couldn't stop laughing, though. I covered my mouth in an attempt to try to be serious, but I couldn't. She stood there with her hands on her hips, looking clueless and confused, so I had to ask. "Ayo, you good?"

"Umm, where we at and how we get back to the house?"

It was a legit question but hell, I wasn't sure either. I sat up and pointed down the street, only to notice that my hands looked like they were floating. I was amazed at how my finger looked as I pointed up the street, unsure of the direction we were supposed to go.

I started to panic because I realized we were lost and had no clue which way the house was. I stood up next to her and I felt like I was walking on the moon. I felt myself slowly rocking back and forth in slow motion. I was looking at her, she was looking at me, and we were both trying to figure out what to do next. I grabbed my phone to FaceTime my sister, not realizing there wasn't much she could do, being that we were states apart.

"Sis, OMG!! Girl, my ass high off that edible we took. We got to get back to the house."

"Ayanna, girl, yo ass too far from home to be taking an edible."

"I know, Sis, but we good. I promise, we good."

"Where y'all at and who y'all with?"

"We with Andre and his brother, Christian, but they not with us right now. They back at the house. Let me call him really quick. I'll call you right back."

"Ok, make sure you call me right back."

I hung up the FT call and attempted to call Christian, but I couldn't dial the number. It took me five attempts to try and get him on the phone. He finally answered.

"Christian!! Where are you? Keyonna and I can't find our way back to the house."

I could hear him giggling on the other end of the phone. I was legit scared and nervous because we really didn't know where we were and how we were going to tell him where we were for them to come get us.

"Turn around," he said.

I slowly turned around to see him coming up the street with Andre. I grabbed Keyonna by the arm and headed in his direction, but we were so high, every time we took two steps forward, it felt like they were getting further away. It felt like we were on one of the funhouse rides where the floor moves. No matter how fast you try to go, you aren't going anywhere at all. I couldn't help but start laughing again but I felt like we were stuck in one spot, even though we were moving. I could see Andre and Christian both laughing hard as hell as they approached us.

"Y'all good?" Andre asked.

"They high as fuck," Christian said to Andre as they grabbed us both and headed back towards the house.

We hadn't eaten anything yet that morning and those edibles hit us fast and hard. We made our way back to the house and sat out on the patio by the pool. I was trying my best to shake the high feeling but the more I closed my eyes, the more it felt like everything around me was spinning.

Keyonna couldn't keep her composure. One minute she would be laughing uncontrollably and the next she would be crying for no reason. I called my sister back to let her know we made it back. She scolded me about getting high out in public in a place I didn't know. I assured her I was okay and hung up to go get ready for dinner. It was our last night in the big, beautiful house in the big, beautiful city. I wasn't sure who suggested it, but it was requested that we all wear black for dinner.

Andre had dinner catered at the house so we wouldn't have to worry about going out. I had this cute little black cocktail dress I packed that I put on, did my hair up and put on some makeup. I wanted to look good for Christian.

It was our last night and I wanted it to be special. When I came down to the dining room, everyone was taking their seats at the table. I looked over at Christian and smiled at him. He was standing behind a chair, motioning for me to come sit.

I looked over at Keyonna and she finally looked like she was back to her normal self. I told myself, I wasn't doing anymore edibles after that day. It took too long to come down from that high.

I sat down next to Christian and looked at us all sitting around the table in our black outfits. We looked like a black mafia family as we sat around and laughed, joked, drank, and ate together. I would always remember that night, that trip, and my new friends.

The next morning, we all got up and stacked our bags by the door for the drivers to load into the cars. Keyonna, Christian and I were flying back to Atlanta, but Andre was staying behind to handle some more business. Keyonna hugged and kissed him goodbye before he got into one of the cars and drove to the house, he would be staying at by himself.

His cousin and his girl hopped into the other car; I wasn't sure where they were going. Whether they were flying out or staying there. They seemed to have been on good terms for a change and I wished them the best.

The three of us got into the truck and headed towards the airport. Christian's flight was before ours, so he headed towards the gate. He stopped and turned towards me to hug me. He kissed me so softly on the lips and told me to call him when I landed, said our goodbyes, and he went on his way.

Keyonna and I still had a few hours before our flight; we grabbed some food and sat and waited. I went over all the events of the last days. The moments I loved the most were the ones with Christian. He had really made me feel something I hadn't felt in a long time: loved and wanted.

Our flight was up next; we checked out bags with TSA and I could hear my phone buzzing right before it went through the scanner. I got to the other side to pull it out and saw it was a call from Trina, the sitter. I called back, thinking something was wrong. She was telling me that she needed to have someone come pick the kids up since she had to start a new job tomorrow and she knew my flight was coming in pretty late.

I called my sister and gave her Trina's info so she could go grab her nieces and nephews. I was so busy trying to get things straight with my kids and my sister that we almost missed the call to board the plane. I grabbed Keyonna's hand and told her to come on.

Once we boarded, we saw that we had separate seats, which was fine. I was just ready to get home to my babies. Once we took off, I leaned my seat back and closed my eyes. It was bittersweet to leave, but I was glad to be heading home.

The landing was rough once we hit Atlanta; it was about 11:45 at night. We grabbed our bags from the overhead bin and headed to baggage claim to get the rest. Keyonna called her mom to come get us from the airport so neither of us would have to spend money on an Uber. While we stood outside and waited for her, I decided to call Christian to let him know we made it back. I was tired as fuck. I just wanted to go home, grab my kids, take a shower, and hit the bed. He picked up after the 4th ring. "Hey, we made it back."

He sounded groggy, like he was asleep already. "Glad you made it okay. Wish you were here with me."

As good as it sounded, I wanted my own bed that night. "I wish I was, too. Listen, our ride is here. I'll hit you tomorrow. Goodnight."

I hung up, grabbed my bag, threw it in the car, and climbed in the back seat. The car ride home was silent. We got to Keyonna's house, I grabbed my things as fast as I could out the trunk, gave her a hug, and hopped in my car and headed to my sister's house.

She told me some of the kids weren't sleep because they knew I was coming and wanted to be awake when I got there. My baby girl, Lisa, waited up for me. My sister and I chatted briefly as we got the kids into the car. I gave her a huge hug and told her that I would call her once I got home. Once we finally got home, I got all the kids in the house, while my baby girl grabbed one of my bags. I got them all in and ran out to grab the last bag.

Once they were all settled into bed, I took a nice, long, hot shower, reminiscing about the shower with Christian in Cali. I stepped out the bathroom and saw all the stuff from some of the bags all over the bed. I was too tired to put anything away. I threw everything to the floor, climbed into bed, and passed smooth out. Home sweet home!

Chapter 6

I barely wanted to open my eyes and get out of bed. I was so exhausted from the late flight. It was a Monday morning and neither me nor the kids wanted anything to do with getting out of bed right then. It was almost ten-thirty and I needed to get us up so we could grab something to eat.

I got them all up and dressed, and made sure they brushed their teeth and washed their faces, even if we didn't shower. I had no energy to cook, so we hopped in the car and went to a restaurant for breakfast.

They were all talking over each other, asking me how my trip was and telling me they missed me and, of course, asking if I brought them anything back. I was just happy to be home. I missed their faces and their smiles.

At the restaurant, the waiter seated all six of us and told us he would be back to take our orders in a minute. As soon as we all got situated, my phone rang. I sat there staring at the number. I knew who it was and what the call was pertaining to. The laughter and smile faded from my face. I dropped my head in an effort to gather my thoughts before I answered.

It was the nurse calling to confirm my son's surgery appointment. "Your son, Deon, is scheduled for surgery on 8-18-20 at eight a.m."

I confirmed all his info, made note of the time and location, and hung up the phone. The food came and I no longer had an appetite. I started thinking about everything I needed to do to prepare for his surgery. Who was going to watch my kids? How long were we going to be there? What if something went wrong? I had a million things shoot through my mind at that moment.

First things first was finding someone to watch his siblings while we were at the hospital, so I started texting people I assumed would watch them all if need be. I posted a cryptic message on Facebook about always having to do things on my own and, not even five minutes later, a friend of mine that I hadn't talk to in a while hit me up on Messenger asking if I was okay. I told her what all was going on and that I was trying to find someone to watch my kids for a couple days and, without hesitation, she offered to help out.

Tiffany and I grew up together, but it had been a while since we'd spoken to one another. Work and kids and having to take care of Deon had all gotten in the way. She told me that she'd changed her number and she texted me her new address and all.

Our kids knew each other and, at first, I told her "no" because I didn't want it to put too much on her, but she insisted. I told her what time I would need to drop the kids off and that it may be a day or two. She didn't care; she was happy to help me out.

After my chat with her, while the kids were finishing up their meals, I spoke with them about what all was going to happen with their brother and what they could expect once the surgery was over. They all looked concerned, but they understood, and they knew it was for the best. After we were done, I paid the bill and we all hopped in the car and headed to Wal-Mart. I needed to pick up a few things for the house and some stuff to take with them to Tiffany's house.

Once we got back to the house, they wanted to stay outside and play for a while. It was nice out, so I let them play; it had been almost a week since they've been home. The trip to Cali seemed so long ago, considering everything I had to focus on right then.

I sat down at the kitchen table and debated if I should call Deon's father. I had to think long and hard about making that call because his father had not been a part of his life since he was born. A few phone calls here and there but he hadn't shown much interest in him at all. However, I figured since he was having surgery, I would at least let him know. I called both his lines; no answer.

I decided to reach out to his mom instead, Mrs. Olivia. I called her to pass along a message to her son, Kenny, about Deon's procedure. I explained everything to her and her response to me was, "Alesha, you will have to talk to him about all of that. I don't want to be in the middle of anything going on between the two of you."

I simply said, "Okay," and hung up the phone.

I could understand his father not wanting to be a part of Deon's life but his grandmother, too? I just didn't get how a family couldn't acknowledge a child at all. Since his father had me blocked on everything, I had to make a new account to get a message to him for him to call me. After ten minutes of that, he finally called me back.

"Hey, Kenny."

He was like, "Wuz up?"

"Well, your son is having surgery in two days. Can you come down to the hospital?"

"Why he having surgery? What's wrong with him now?"

I moved the phone away and took a deep breath; like this stupid motherfucker, did you not just hear what the hell I said? So, I placed the phone back on my ear. "You know it's his legs, Kenny. I messaged you about it before. You know what? If you're coming, just let me know. If not, cool. You still haven't come to see him at all anyway, so I was just letting you know."

He said, "Alright then. Just let me know how his surgery go," and hung up.

All I could do was shake my head at it all. How could he be so cold-hearted and have so many excuses to not come see his child? I tried to shake it off but, between him and his mama, I couldn't get it out of my head how they had not a care in the world for Deon.

I started getting the kids clothes together. I packed about three days' worth of stuff for the girls and only a day or two for Deon. I figured he would be in the hospital gown for the majority of his stay, so there was no need to pack a bunch of clothes for him. I made sure to put his favorite toy in the bag; something familiar to keep him calm and less nervous about being there.

I called Christian to see what he was up to. I needed to clear my head some kind of way and I knew talking to him was just what I needed. He picked up on the second ring.

"Hey, Christian. What you doing later?"

"Nothing. I'm out right now taking care of some business. Why? What's up? You okay?"

I said, "Well, I'm a little stressed and I need someone to talk to and clear my mind a bit."

He said, "Okay. Well, meet me at my house in an hour. If I'm not there, get the key from the little space behind the mailbox and go in and wait for me."

"Alright, cool. See you in a few."

I grabbed some night clothes for me and the kids, and I yelled downstairs for Amber to tell her sisters to put their shoes on so we could head out. It took about an hour to get to Christian's house from there, but I didn't care. I was ready for him to hug me and hold me. Little did he know, he was my peace of mind and my go-to when everything felt so bottled up inside of me.

I got the kids together and packed their bags and everything into the car. I stopped for gas near the corner and grabbed some snacks for them inside the store. The whole drive over, I kept thinking about Kenny and the conversations with him and his mom earlier. I wanted to try to forget about them and focus on Deon and his surgery. I had too much on my plate as it was to be worried about a man that hadn't taken care of him a day in his life. I did everything for my kids with no help from him or anyone in his family.

Some days it bothered me and others, I couldn't have cared less, but with his surgery, I would've assumed that they would've had a little more compassion and they didn't. So, you know what? Fuck 'em both!

The GPS got me to his house in a little under an hour. He had left the light on in the driveway for me, but he was actually pulling up with me at the same time. He let the garage door open, then pulled in, and I pulled into the other side. He helped me get the kids out the car and gave me a big hug. I swear, in that moment, I felt like a load was lifted off my shoulders and I didn't want to let go.

He must have felt that something was wrong. He took a step back and looked down at me. "You okay? What's wrong?"

"Man, there's so much that I'm about to go through, I don't know if I'm coming or going today."

He replied, "Come on; let's talk."

He helped me get the kids and the bags out of the car and we headed inside. I walked in and admired how nice and neat his house was for a single man. Everything was in its place and I was in awe at how nicely furnished it all was. I took my shoes off by the door and told the kids to do the same.

He turned the T.V. on for the kids and told them to make themselves at home in the living room. He grabbed my hand and led me up the stairs and down the hall to his bedroom. I sat down on the foot of the bed while he rolled up at a small table he had in the corner.

"Come on. Talk to me. What's going on with you, babe?"

"Well, you know my son has his surgery date coming up."

He said, "Yeah. You good with that?"

"Well, now his dad not trying to show up or be supportive at all and I'm gonna need some help with my baby. I have to tend to my other kids with school and just other things around the house, so I don't know what to do, Christian. I feel so overwhelmed with the thought of it all."

He said, "Well, look, I'm here if you need me. I can come to the hospital with you, if you want me to be there. I have no problem being there for you, if you need support. I can try to help with the kids, if you need that, too. Just tell me what it is you need, and I got you."

I sat there, thinking to myself, *Where on earth did this man come from?*

He was prepared to step in and be there for kids that weren't even his, but I couldn't see myself putting that type of pressure on him, so I replied, "That's cool. I would appreciate that, but I want to be by myself at the hospital, if his dad can't be there. I really do appreciate the support, but I have to deal with this on my own. I mean, this is not his first surgery, but I'm hoping this is the last. I'm just in my feelings that this will be my baby's sixth surgery and his dad has not attended one yet. I mean, after that many, I'm used to being there by myself. It's just the fact that every time he has to go through this, his father doesn't seem to care at all. I'm going to pray my way through like every other time."

Christian said, "Babe, you're a good mother to your kids and you're strong, so I know you will be okay. You can call me anytime if you change your mind about me being there, so don't stress it, aight? I'm here."

I looked at him and smiled. "Thanks, but I'm good. I just needed to vent to somebody for a bit."

"Yeah, well, it's all good. Go ahead and jump in the shower and get comfortable. I'll run the water for you. When you get out, get in the bed and relax."

I was so tense and tight, I needed a moment to myself to breathe. I stayed in the shower longer than I usually would. It was so relaxing. I had a flashback about the shower we'd taken in Cali. A small part of me had wished he had come in there with me, but the other part was kind of happy he didn't.

By the time I got out, all the kids were asleep. Christian had put them in the bed while I was in the shower. I slipped on my pajama shorts and tank top and crawled into his big bed. I laid back and turned on the TV, flipping through the channels trying to find a movie to put on while I waited for Christian to come to bed. I was so at peace and relaxed, I drifted off to sleep.

I woke up at 10:27 a.m., got dressed, and got my kids up. I came back in the room and tapped Christian on his shoulder. "Hey, I'm finna go. I will call you when I make it home."

He said, "Okay. Let me walk you to the door."

"No, it's okay. Go back to sleep. I'll lock the bottom lock on my way out."

I kissed him on his forehead and slowly closed the

door to his room on the way out. Not sure what was in the plans for us, but I was surely grateful for a man like him.

Shawdae

Chapter 7

On the drive home, all I could think about was what was going to happen over the next few days. I was nervous about everything going as planned, as well as hoping that the surgery would have a great outcome. I took time out to make sure I prayed to God about everything and asked for the strength to get me through it all. I was trying not to let the worrying consume me but couldn't help it.

Soon as we got home, I fed the kids and told them to try not to bug me too much. The older kids were in their rooms with TV and books and what-not to keep them occupied. I couldn't help but to want Deon under me, but he seemed to be out of it; almost as if he knew what was going to happen tomorrow. I put him to bed and went up to my room and dozed off.

I rolled over and looked at the clock and saw that it was 4:30 a.m. I feel like I had just fallen asleep and not it was time for me to get up and put on a strong face. I got up and got myself dressed and all the bags together. When I was ready, I got the rest of the kids up and started getting them dressed. The twins were dragging so I got the two oldest, Amber and Crystal, to help them get dressed. I left Deon in his pajamas. They would be changing him into a hospital gown anyway. I packed all the kids and the bags into the car, and we headed towards Tiffany's house.

I didn't even turn any music on; just drove in silence. The kids were still half-sleep from it being so early and plus, I wanted to keep a clear head. My phone rang and part of me had wished it was Kenny saying that he would meet me at the hospital, but it was Tiffany checking to see if I was still dropping the kids off to her. I told her that I was already on the road heading her way.

After thirty minutes of driving, I made it to her house. I dropped the kids off and handed her some money, gave them all kisses, and hopped back on the road. I didn't want to be late for his surgery because I didn't want to have to reschedule. I had finally prepared my mind for it, so I wanted to hurry up and get it over with. I prayed about it and I was hopeful that after his surgery, he would at least be able to stand, let alone walk. It had been two years and he hadn't been able to do any of it.

The closer to the hospital I got, the more nervous I was becoming. I was trying my best to remain calm for his sake. I didn't want him to see how nervous I was and cause him to panic. I was on edge about them putting him to sleep. It was not the first time, but every time put me on edge. I parked the car, grabbed him and his bags and headed inside.

He was so sleepy still; all I could do was hold him close and squeeze him tight. I cuddled him the whole time we sat in the waiting area. When I signed him, I noticed he was third on the list. After about ten minutes of waiting, they came out and called his name. I followed the nurse through the double doors and into what would be his room for the next few days. Room 14 was cold and silent. She handed me a small yellow gown for me to change Deon into. She asked me a few questions so they could get him registered in the system. When she walked out, two doctors came in to go over the procedure, but before I knew it, five more had come in to explain their various roles in the surgery.

It was too much to process, but I sat and listened to each of them attentively. They all left out and the nurse came back and asked if I had any questions. The only thing I wanted to know was how long the whole thing would take. When she told me six hours, my mouth dropped, and my heart felt like it hit the bottom of my stomach. What was I going to do for six hours, besides worry to death about what was going on in there?

I had to stay focused, though. I held his hand as he lay on the bed and prayed as we waited for them to come take him away. I shed a tear as I kissed him on the cheek; if only he had more people by his bedside. His father at least should've been there, but there was nothing I could do about that. I was there and that's all that mattered.

They came in to take him away and I followed behind the bed down the hall as long as I could before I couldn't go any further. I had six hours to kill and wasn't sure what I was going to do while I waited. I went down to the cafeteria to grab some breakfast. I sat at the table with my phone and texted a few people and made a couple calls and realized the time wasn't moving.

I found a chair in the hall and curled up in it to try and get some sleep. When I woke up, four hours had passed by. I jumped up to get an update from the nurse and she told me that he was doing fine and it shouldn't be too much longer. I walked outside to get some air before going back to his room to wait for them to bring him in.

As soon as I got up to his room and go situated, my phone started to buzz. It was Christian. "Hey, how's everything going? How you holding up?"

"I'm good", I replied. "Just waiting on him to come out of surgery. Should be soon."

"Okay, cool. Do you need anything, shorty?"

Of course, I said "no." I didn't need nor want anything at the moment except for my child to come out of a successful surgery.

"Okay then, babe. If you need anything, call me. Aight?"

"Yes, thanks for calling and checking on me. I appreciate that."

"Anytime. Talk to you later."

Any other time, I would've sat on the phone with him and chatted longer, but I wasn't much for words.

"Ms. Evans, the procedure is done, and your son will be coming out soon."

I was happy to hear those words. She explained that they were going to be putting him in a different room on the PICU floor. So, I gathered all of his things and followed her up to his new room. They were already getting him settled in before I could get there. I walked in and all I could do was cry. I wanted to hold him so bad, but I was afraid to even touch him, thinking I would hurt him. I took a picture and sent it to both Kenny's fat ass and his mama. Even though she told me she wanted nothing to do with her grandson, I still updated her anyway. I really wasn't expecting a reply from either of them, but to my surprise, she messaged me back.

"AMEN. God is good."

She asked what hospital we were at. I gave her the name of the hospital and the room number, so she had no excuse to not come visit. We would be there for about a week, so she had time to come see him if she wanted.

He texted me back, talking about tell my son I love him, and I'll see him soon. My face immediately turned sour, and I erased his message. He should've been there at the hospital with him. "Fuck you," I said under my breath. Kenny and I were together for six years and it took me two years to convince him that Deon was his and he needed to try to be a part of his life. He kept saying Deon wasn't his. We argued and fought so much over it and, eventually, I came to terms with the fact that he wasn't interested in being in his life. He had other kids that he was there for, but despite everything we went through, he refused to be there for mine.

We'd been there for three days and all I wanted to do was get some real sleep. They'd come in every five minutes, wanting to check his vitals and give him pain meds. I reached out to Kenny to see if he would come sit with him a little while so I could at least run home to shower and check on the other kids. He kept talking in circles since he was around his other baby mama. I told myself, I simply wasn't going to bother anymore with him.

His mother never came to visit neither and I hadn't heard from her since the first day I texted her. It had just been me there sitting with him, trying to keep him calm and in good spirits. My sister called to check on us, of course. She asked how everything was and if we'd had any real food since being there. I told her "no," so she said she was going to order food and have it sent to the hospital for us. It was the little things like that that made the stay a little easier.

Christian also called a few times, always checking to see if I needed anything. I always said "no" but that I appreciated his calls.

I would sit by the window at night and rock Deon in my arms as I watched all the cars come and go in and out the garage. Part of me was hoping that just one time, one of those cars would be his father. I held him tight and close so he could feel all the love I had to give him; even the extra love I knew he deserved from his father.

All that I was going through lately was making me such a stronger person. It was basically a test of my patience and my strength. Just knowing I could get through all that alone and not lose my mind. I could either sit and cry about it or suck it up and handle it all like a boss… I chose the latter

of the two.

Chapter 8

After being there almost a whole week, only a few people had called to check on me and Deon. One of them being Kenny's best friend's mom, Ciara. She called and checked in on Deon all the time, as if he were one of her own grandkids.

She came to visit us on that Thursday. It was nice to have her there, talking and asking what she could do to help. His own grandmother didn't even bother to come visit. Yet, there was this woman offering me help in any way I needed.

I watched her as she stood over Deon holding his hand and talking to him as he smiled back at her. I saw her close her eyes and pray for him. I only wished that his actual family would be so loving, but that was just as good, and I was grateful that she cared enough to be there with us.

A few nurses had come in with a ton of paperwork and began explaining about the physical therapy he would need. They provided a small wheelchair for him to get around in while we were there and told me about how I could get one for home if I needed it. I was getting excited because I thought we would be going home that day... until the doctor came in and explained that they thought it would be best if he stayed one more night. I felt crushed, like seriously. I wanted to go home, sleep in my own bed, and see my other children.

Ciara saw the look on my face and told me, "Don't worry. Let them take care of him as much as needed. He will be fine enough to go home soon."

I felt so overwhelmed, sitting there in the room knowing that I had other children to tend to and wanted to be home with them all. Ciara assured me it would all be okay and to take it easy on myself. She had to go but I wanted her to stay longer. She told me if I needed her for anything to call her, no matter what it was. I appreciated her for that.

As she was leaving out, room service was coming in to bring Deon his dinner. I sat him up and got him ready to eat. I fed him, gave him a sponge bath, played a few games with him, and smothered him with kisses until he fell asleep. Once I knew he was good and sleep, I went and took myself a much-needed shower. I took the moment to breathe easy and told myself we would be home soon, and our lives could get back to some type of normalcy.

As I was getting out, Christian called and asked if I wanted to grab something to eat and get out for a minute to clear my head. I told him "no." I wanted to stay there with my baby. He understood and didn't press the issue. We spoke for a few more minutes and then said goodnight to one another. I turned my phone off curled up next to Deon and tried my best to get some sleep.

Friday came and I was up and already packing our things to leave. I asked the nurse how soon we could go; she said as soon as she printed out his prescriptions and discharge papers. I waited patiently for thirty minutes.

She finally came back in and said, "Okay, let's remove this IV and get him out of here."

She handed me all his paperwork, I put my baby in the wheelchair and flew out of that place as fast as I could without looking back. I was glad to be going home!

I had to adjust a lot of things at home for Deon. He was only able to sit up in his brace for thirty minutes a day in the wheelchair. Tiffany dropped the kids off to me and before i knew it the whole house was hectic and chaotic. It was nice to be home and having all my kids there, but it soon became a bit overwhelming with them and Deon. Trying to care for him in the midst of getting them to and from school, setting up and taking Deon to his doctor's appointments was becoming a bit of a challenge with no other support. I was determined to make it through the week; the grocery shopping, cooking, cleaning, and helping with homework. I was proving to myself that I was stronger than I gave myself credit for. Trying to pursue my acting career was pushed to the back burner. I simply had no time to dedicate to it those days. On top of that, Deon's birthday was approaching fast.

There were still no calls or texts from Kenny since we'd been home. I didn't even bother to text him either because I simply did not want to deal with the nonchalant attitude he had about everything that I was dealing with.

I wasn't sure what kind of party to do for Deon because he was still inside his back brace and would have to be held a certain way in order to be able to enjoy himself. But with everything he had been through, I wanted to make sure his day was special. I was thinking a big party in the park with a moonbounce. I sent Kenny a text to see if he would like to contribute in some way, but it went ignored like all the others.

A few days later, Ciara hit my line to tell me that Kenny gave her a message that he would pay for everything and to let him know how much everything would be. He still would not communicate directly with me, so all the miscommunication between us and messages not being translated right through her caused all the plans I had for his birthday to go left. I gave up and eventually decided to throw him a party at Chuck E. Cheese. I got him two cakes, invited a few friends, and left it at that.

The day of the party, everyone showed up to celebrate and support Deon for his big day. One of the mamas of one of Kenny's other friends came as well with her grandkids: Miss Angela. Kenny apparently called her to say that he would be pay me for the decorations and everything. I paid it no mind at that point. He'd do whatever it was that he was gonna do and I left it at that.

Everyone was enjoying themselves and having a good time when Miss Angela got a call to her phone. Kenny had called her to let her know that he was outside and wanted someone to come out and get Deon's gifts from the car. I was really confused as to why he didn't bring them inside himself. It was obvious that he was ashamed of the condition his son had and was afraid to face it, but there was still no excuse to come that far and not even come in to see him.

I didn't want to spoil the day with my attitude about it, so I had Miss Angela send some of my cousins out to the car to get the gifts and left it at that. The kids were having a good time. We sang "Happy Birthday," and ate, and it was good seeing Deon in such good spirits.

I had several things I wanted to say to Kenny and plenty of questions that only he could answer. As much as I wanted to get it off my chest at that moment, I didn't want to put a damper on the rest of the party.

Miss Angela was looking through the bags Kenny sent inside. "Oh, look at this. That was nice of his daddy to get him some clothes and a pair of shoes."

Everyone's eyes were on me looking for a reaction. I had to control my face and smile but, on the inside, I was screaming, "ONE PAIR OF SHOES AND THREE OUTFITS!! THIS NIGGA!!!"

I was not about to praise him for doing the bare minimum after all that I was doing for Deon. We finished going through the rest of the gifts and Miss Angela and I were trying to get everything together to put into my car. She motioned for me to come over to her, so I walked over, thinking she maybe wanted me to get something for her, but instead, she wanted to talk to me about Kenny.

"Be thankful for what he gave, baby."

I laughed like, "Are you serious?"

Before I could say anything else, she said, "He wants to see his son and he will. He just needs time to get himself together, hon. He's been trying to help his mom get her catering business started so he's been busy with that, along with trying to get on his own feet."

"People keep finding excuses for him to not step up and be responsible, but whatever. I'm not about to get into all of that today."

I cut the conversation short and walked away. It was almost time for us to go. I passed out the rest of the cake and started cleaning up. Everyone helped me bring the things to my car. My baby said he had a great time, so as long as he was happy, I was happy.

The next morning, I got a text from an unknown number saying: **WUZ UP?**

I called it but got no answer. I was sitting there trying to figure out who could it be texting me from an unknown number. So, I replied: **WHO DIS?**

This Kenny. we need to talk!

I sat there and shook my head like, *What does he want now?*

All of a sudden, he wanted to talk to me. I really wasn't in the mood, but I replied back: **What do you want to talk about now?**

No reply for about ten minutes and then he called. I answered the phone and he immediately began to go off on me about how he couldn't deal with me, my attitude, and my bullshit. He wanted to have a relationship with his son but didn't want to deal with me in order to do so.

I sat there listening to him go on and on, taking it all in because when it was my turn to speak, I was going to go all the way off on the fool. So, I was letting him get it all out and all off his chest without interruption. He finally stopped talking and there was my opportunity to say what all it was I felt I needed to say.

"Let me tell you something, nigga. You are completely full of shit! Kenny, you have been out here living your best damn life and now that shit's starting to catch up to you, you have the audacity to want to go off on somebody else and point the finger and place blame for your own shit!" He tried to cut me off. "Shut up and let me finish. I have spoken nothing but facts when it came to you and I've always been truthful to those who've asked about our relationship. But it's not about us, it's about our son. He needs both of his parents. You walked out six months before he was even born and still completely fail to acknowledge publicly that he belongs to you. You left me to take care of him alone. A child YOU asked for me to keep and once you found out he had a condition, you completely disregarded him as your own. You didn't even want to tell your mama that I was even pregnant. Talking about just wait till I tell everybody, when all it was, was you trying to get me to stay quiet about it and hide him from everybody. I don't know who you think I am, but I am not that type of female. As soon as I started telling people and speaking my truth, you want to go around and start telling people I'm crazy and this, that and the third. I'm over here taking care of OUR disabled child. Surgeries, physical therapy, and doctor's appointments all with you not giving a damn. And the child support you call yourself sending is barely enough to do anything with, so don't call me with your bullshit today because you really need to check yourself. You need to grow the fuck up and be a father to your son because right now you are a tired, poor, pathetic excuse of a man."

I guess I hit a major nerve with everything I had to say, and he started to yell and cuss at me. I simply hung up the phone. I didn't know who he thought he was calling me up the way he did after not even bothering to show his face yesterday at Deon's birthday party. I was all for having a conversation for the right reason but what you were not going to do was call me up and try to bash me and shame me for doing my job as a mother. When I realized that Deon had a condition, I knew that my life as a mother of five was going to change drastically. I would have to step it up as a mother and go hard as fuck for mine and I wasn't about to let some deadbeat-ass baby father tell me that I wasn't doing my job right. He couldn't even show up when it was necessary but came at me like I owed him something. All the back and forth, the arguing, blocking and unblocking of numbers, and all of that was starting to get really tired really quick. Allowing him to take me out of character wasn't going to help me in the moments when I needed to be at my best. So, fuck him. I'd gotten through all of that shit so far without his help and I wasn't about to beg for his help now. I had me, I had us and nothing or nobody was going to take away from that.

Chapter 9

It continued to be a bit of a struggle to tend to the other kids while actively trying to assist Deon with his needs. Over the next few weeks, Kenny and I attempted to have other conversations, but we really weren't seeing eye to eye on much of anything. As much as I would have liked for him to be there and be the man my son needed, I knew deep down he would never be what Deon needed.

There was even an attempt to have a conversation with Kenny's mother, Ms. Olivia, but that didn't go over so well either. It was like we were trying but it wasn't getting anywhere. In a last attempt at trying to make amends, I reached out to Miss Angela to try to set something up between Kenny and me. She said that she would try her best. She couldn't promise anything but said she would at least try.

I was sitting in one of Deon's doctor's appointments when my phone began going off. I ignored it because his visit was way more important than whoever was trying to reach me. The doctor was going on about how much therapy he would need to be able to walk and I was agreeing to it all. Whatever my baby needed to do to ensure that he would be able to walk around like a normal child, I was all in. My phone was steady ringing and going off, but I was intent on signing all the paperwork to get Deon set up with his appointments with the Pediatric Orthopedist and all the other therapies he had to receive.

I was excited to be able to start the next leg of this journey because I wanted so badly for my son to start walking. I left the appointment with so much hope and happiness. The doctors were very optimistic about how well everything would work out.

I strapped Deon in his seat and got in to check my messages. I saw missed calls from Miss Angela and some texts for me to call her. So, I called her back. "Miss Angela, is everything okay? I was in with Deon's doctor; that's why I couldn't answer. What's going on?"

She informed me that Kenny was trying to reach me and that he agreed to finally have a conversation. I thought to myself, *Okay, let's go into this with an open mind, not jump to any conclusion, and try to hear him out.*

Soon as I got home, I got Deon settled and grabbed my phone out my purse. I didn't even read the text messages he sent. I took a deep breath and dialed the number. As the phone rang, I kept telling myself to keep cool and don't trip. Kenny answered and, by the tone of his voice, I already knew it was going to be some fuck shit.

"Ayo, Alesha, why the fuck you still got me on child support? That's some bullshit! You a bitch, you stupid ass hoe! That's why I don't even wanna see my son because you do too damn much, and I don't be wanting to deal witcho dumb ass. I will see him when I feel like seeing him. I can't deal with you, man!!"

I interrupted. "Nigga, you gotta be fucking kidding me. THIS is what you been blowing my phone up about?

Take you off child support? You don't do shit as it is; that's the LEAST you can do. Ain't no way in hell I'm taking you off! You barely even know him, and you've only seen him in pictures. Do better and maybe I'll think about it!"

He went on to tell me that if I took him off, I would get more. He assumed that I was about to take his word that he would give me money directly without me going through the courts. I think the fuck not. I told him all I wanted was for him to be there for Deon and for him to know his other siblings. How I needed for us to be able to communicate so that we could coparent and raise him together.

He wasn't trying to hear any of that though; he was only trying to plead his case to get me to take him off support. He started calling me names and screaming into the phone. All I could do was hang up and block him at that point. He was one rude ass, fat fucker to come at me the way that he did. You would think being the mother of his one and only son, that he would've been a little more involved. I couldn't let his ignorance drain me and keep me from doing what I had to do. You would think his mother would get on him about doing better, but she was no help either. How could they sleep at night, knowing there was a child out there with special needs that they simply didn't care for?

His mother would always point the finger at me, and place blame my way as if he had nothing at all to do with the situation. There he was living with his other baby mother, Myesha, and their daughter. To be honest, I wasn't even sure if she knew who I was or that he had a son with me. The house they lived in, I didn't even know they shared it because every time I had went over there, he was always there with his homeboys and she was never around. Come to find out he had two houses and if she wasn't at that one with him, she was at the other.

He was good at hiding things, so it would've been no surprise if he'd kept Deon from her. Even though I fought with myself about it, I decided to call Myesha and let her know what was going on. The woman in me wanted to have a talk with her woman-to-woman to see if she would have any influence over him being a better father to our son. That call didn't prove to be any help at all.

Apparently, whatever it was he told her, she believed all of it. She didn't believe that Deon belonged to Kenny and she didn't want her child around mine. I let her talk to hear what all she had to say before I said anything back. She went on and on about how he told her that I was a liar and all this other stuff.

By the time she got done, I didn't even have the energy to reply. I simply told her to believe what she wanted to but that she could ask anybody around about us. He tried to hide me and the baby from his mom, his sister, and even her, but yet she still believed whatever he wanted her to believe. All of them, like they were brainwashed or something. Even his mother, Ms. Olivia, and I had had a few words about the whole situation and she had threatened to call the police and press charges if I didn't stop calling her phone. I tried my best to make amends where I could, but everybody was on their own bullshit about it. I wanted so much to be able to let it go, but I couldn't. I wanted them to acknowledge my son. Was that too much to even ask?

His sister, Latina, was also putting in her two cents. I couldn't stand her; she was so disrespectful towards me without even hearing my side of things, of course. It was kind of hard to avoid her since we shopped at some of the same places and even got our hair done at the same shop. I attempted to reach out to her once and she snapped at me about bothering her mom. She told me to stop texting her before her and I had a real problem; that neither her nor her mama wanted anything to do with Kenny and my mess.

I had to correct her. Deon was not "mess." He was a child that no one seemed to care about except me. She knew her brother was a hoe out in the streets and that he was going around making babies with whomever would sleep with him, but then pay them afterwards to keep quiet about it. She knew but still wasn't interested in hearing anything I had to say. She basically told me that if he wanted to bring his son around, then he would but, until then, I should fuck off and leave them all alone. So, you know what? I did… I finally let it go.

I ran into one of his friends from high school while out and about one day. Her name was Destiny. They had been friends all throughout school and even till that day, she was like his right-hand man. When he and I first met, she was around. She wouldn't hesitate to call him on his bullshit if she saw him moving wrong. When she found out I was pregnant, she was telling him to make sure he did the right thing by me.

So, when I ran into her, we got to talking and I thought maybe she could talk to him about the situation but, even in knowing he was wrong, she still tried to play the "but he's a good dude" card. She used to check on me in the beginning, when I first had Deon, but then the calls stopped. She mentioned she would hit me up soon, but I figured that I probably wouldn't hear from her after that day. I made up my mind right then and there that I wouldn't bother to communicate with anyone else regarding Kenny. After trying for two years just to get him to acknowledge Deon and be there for him, I was going to let it go and let the chips fall where they lay. I couldn't force him to do anything he didn't want and even though I would never understand it, I knew that anything I wanted from Kenny, I wasn't going to get.

Months had gone by and I would get messages from unknown numbers asking if Deon was okay. I knew it was Kenny and I ignored them. I didn't want to play any games with him and knew that if I replied or engaged, it would end in an argument and I was in no mood to be doing any arguing or fighting at that point. He thought the world revolved around him and that he could pick and choose when he wanted to be involved or not. If I could have, I would have dug a hole for that nigga and had him dive right into it. I blocked his number and even took down all of Deon's pictures because I refused to allow him to watch Deon grow up through social media. I didn't even want to give him that satisfaction. I even had to cut Miss Angela off because she was starting to get caught up in the middle of it all, like she was keeping shit going for her own personal entertainment, so I had to block her also.

Things were becoming overwhelming, with all of Deon's appointments and trying to keep our heads above water. I was starting to miss some of them and having to reschedule them over and over was beginning to eat me up inside. There I was trying so hard to get Kenny to be involved that I wasn't even doing my part anymore. After he missed his fifth appointment, I was pissed about it all because now it came down to the lawyers to determine if they were going to release the disability money for Deon. The missed appointments didn't look good on my part. I felt like my back was against the wall and I was struggling trying to keep the money flowing. I was trying to make it look easy for those looking in from the outside when, in reality, I was falling apart on the inside. I was telling myself I didn't need family or a man to help me and my kids, that I had it under control. I was thankful we had a roof over our heads, and I had a car to get around in, but I needed to do more to be able to provide for my kids. I was sinking into a deep hole that I needed to pull myself out of. I not only cut ties with Kenny and his family but some of my own so-called friends, even Christian. I couldn't have any distractions while I was trying to get my shit together.

I went back to doing nails out of my place to bring in some extra cash. I went to school for it so I figured I might as well make use of the craft. I had my babies to think about so anything I had to do, I did it. I had to get focused and clear my head of the negativity. I was a single mom with little to no help, so it was up to me to provide for them; for us.

It had been a while since I had a break. I still thought about Cali from time to time, but getting another break like that wasn't going to be anytime soon. After thinking about that, I decided that I would dig in my bag of tricks and start trying to act again. I didn't know how I would even make it to auditions because I couldn't leave Deon with anyone, but I prayed on it and asked God to give me strength and make a way. I made sure to keep my thoughts positive and to speak things into existence and, before I knew it, the auditions started to roll in. I knew that things would start to change for me. I just needed to get through the storm before I could get to the blessings on the other side of it all.

Chapter 10

I had a few friends keep their eyes open for me as far as auditions went and as soon as something came up that I was interested in, I called my girlfriend, Sheila, to come watch the kids for me. I didn't have much money to pay her, but I knew once it started to roll in again, I would pay her first.

My boy, Andre, sent me a movie roll he came across that he thought I would be good for. He said it was "TODAY." I had no idea how I was going to even make it there. I had no gas in my car, no money, and I had to get Sheila to watch the kids. I called her as soon as I got the info from him and, like always, she said "no problem." I wasn't sure how I was going to make things work when, all of a sudden, I got a notification that child support had been paid. God was on my side that day. It wasn't much, but enough to put gas in the car and get us where we needed to go. As sorry as that man was, he at least came through on that part. Not by choice, of course, but it was still right on time.

I told the kids, "Listen up. I need you guys to get dressed and be ready by the time Mommy showers and gets dressed. I have an audition and need to get out of here fast. Can you guys do that for me?"

They all answered in unison, "Yes!"

So, I hopped in the shower and my phone was going off with messages. I was in a rush and had no time to stop to check anything.

I hopped out the shower and grabbed my phone to check it while I was pulling clothes from the closet; it was my ex. I tossed my phone on the bed because I meant what I said about staying focused and I knew he ain't want nothing but to waste my damn time. I found something to throw on, packed up some lunches and snacks for the kids, and loaded everyone in the car. It wasn't going to take long to get to her and the place I needed to go to actually wasn't that far from her. With Deon's condition, I wasn't too crazy about leaving him with just anybody, but Sheila I trusted. I had known her for a while; met her through a mutual friend and we clicked. I knew they would be good with her so whenever I had to do anything, audition, shop, or anything I couldn't take Deon along with, I could rely on her to step in when I needed her to.

When we arrived, I explained where I had to go, how long I might be, and what all I had to do. She said, "No worries, girl. Go do your thang and good luck!"

She gave me a big hug and I hopped back in my car and headed to my next destination. I was nervous but, in my mind, I was telling myself not to be worried about anyone else; to breathe and focus on what I needed to do to get the part.

When I got there, I had to park a block over and walk to the building. It was warm out and so many people were out there, and a lot of shops were open, even in the middle of the pandemic. People were still out there working and hustling in Atlanta and there I was arriving to stake my claim in it all. As I approached the building, I peeped the scene; everyone was out there cooling. They had a snack stand, music playing, and people standing around all practicing their lines. After grabbing a script and finding a spot, I ran into a young lady named Asia. She was a music artist and we got to talking and stuff and decided we would run our lines with each other. She was mad cool; we were laughing at the fact that there was only one female role that all those chicks were out there fighting for that one single role. We both agreed that no matter what happened, we would do our best and root for one another.

Little did she know, inside I was rooting for her to get it. I read the script and thought that she would actually be a great fit for the part. I still went through with the audition, obviously, and after we were both done, we hung around and took a few pictures. We were even able to get a few pics with a couple of celebrities that came through the audition area.

Asia and I exchanged numbers and said we would keep in contact with one another. It was crazy that I had just met her but felt like I had known her for years. I guess that's what happens when you meet genuine people with a good heart.

It was late and she offered to give me a ride to my car since I had to park a block away. She was telling me about her single she was trying to push, so I told her to send me her song and I would check it out and promote it for her on my social media pages. She dropped me to my car and told her good luck again on hopefully getting the part. She blew me a kiss and drove off.

I noticed my back left tire looked a little different, but I jumped in my car and prayed that I would make it safe to Shelia's house to get the kids. I was trying to get there as quick as I could because I had this gut feeling that something wasn't right. I just couldn't put my finger on it.

Once I pulled up to Sheila's house, I got the kids together and had a quick conversation with Sheila about the audition. I thanked her again, put the kids in the car, gave her a huge hug, and headed on home. Once I hit the highway, I noticed a strong smell and loud noise coming from the car, but I didn't panic. I pulled over to the right side of the road, put my gun on my hip, and told the kids to stay in the car while I got out to see what the hell the noise was. I walked around and looked at the back of my car and it was my left tire; it had blown out. Just what the fuck I needed right now, man, damn! I called roadside assistance and the police came to make sure everything was okay in the meantime. I assured them that we were fine, but my mind was racing as to who I could call to at least get us home. I went through my call log and called the last few people I had spoken with: Sheila and my sister Ayanna. However, since Sheila was closer to me, she said she would come and pick me and the kids up to make sure we got home safe. I was hesitant to ask her, being that it was late and, plus, she had watched my kids all day, but she was happy to come get us. She told me not to worry and asked exactly where we were. I told her about ten minutes from my house on 85-South.

She said, "Don't worry. I'm on my way."

I got back in the car and waited for Sheila to arrive. I was trying my best to keep cool and stay positive, but I couldn't help but to feel like every time I got ten steps ahead, the devil pulled me back five. I couldn't let it get the best of me, though; I had way more things to be worried about than a tire. That was an easy fix. I was concentrating on making it to all the other auditions I had coming up.

The officer that was sitting behind me pulled up next to my window and informed me that he would be leaving since the tow truck was there. I thanked him for his help and sat in the car and waited for Sheila to arrive. She showed up about three minutes later and me and the kids hopped out of the car and piled into hers. She waited until the tow truck had my car on the lift before pulling off.

"Tonight has been something else, Sheila. Thank you for coming."

She replied, "Oh, girl, don't worry about it. Can't be out here stranded with these babies on the side of the road. I got you."

Once we got home, I put the kids to bed, showered, and crawled into mine; I was exhausted. The tow truck dropped the car to my place, and I would have to figure out where to get it fixed from there, but tonight was not the time to worry about it. I'd figure that shit out in the morning.

I was short on cash after having to come up with money to pay for the first tow. I still needed to get my car from my place to a shop so they could fix my tire. The tow truck driver told me that I needed two tires because the other one was worn down and would probably blow out like the one did last night. I hit up one of my cousins to borrow some extra cash in the meantime but was calling around to find where to get two used tires from for a decent price. I kept telling myself things were going to work out in the end and this was just a small bump in the road. I had an audition in five days and I was going to make it there by any means. I was determined to be on T.V. and I had a good feeling about everything that was getting ready to come my way. I had been submitting my tapes and resumes for different parts and I just knew that one of them was going to come through for me. I could feel it in my soul.

I had three days before I could get my truck back on the road so, in the meantime, I was at home staying busy. Asia, the girl I met at the last audition, hit me up to tell me about the video she was shooting for her single and asked if I wanted to be in it.

"Hell yea!!!" I told her.

She gave me all the details about it, and I told her that I would definitely be there Thursday.

Lucky for me, the mechanic said my truck would be ready for pick up Thursday morning at ten, which was perfect being that her shoot wasn't until seven that night. I swear, it felt like I had a million and one things to do before then and not having a car felt like it was going to be impossible to get everything done. I called up a friend of mine to ask if he would take me to pick my car up in the morning. I didn't call Anthony for much, but whenever I did, he was happy to help me out.

The next morning, I was up early and ready to get my day started. I was excited to pick up my truck and hit the shoot later with Asia.

I hit Ant up to see if he was up and ready, but before I could even ask him anything, he said to me, "Yes, I'm up and I'm ready. Just waiting on you." We both laughed. "You know I'm an early bird. I'll be there in ten minutes, if you ready."

"Okay, Ant. Yes, I'm ready. See you when you get here."

I hung up, grabbed my socks and shoes and my sweater, and headed out the door. Soon as I got downstairs, he was pulling up.

"Damn, what you do? Speed over here?"

He laughed. "Nah, you know my Charger is fast."

"I see you still don't know how to treat a lady. You not going to get out and open the door for me?" He laughed it off and motioned for me to hurry up and get in. "See, that's why you still single, Ant."

He said, "Well, shit, so are you so what you doing wrong?"

"Oh, baby, I'm fine being single. I'm better off that way so I can stay focused on what I got to do." I sat back and talked about the video shoot later while we drove to the shop. "You should send some of your female friends over there tonight, too."

"Now, Alesha, you know I don't do female friends like that. I ain't sending nobody nowhere."

"Well, that's where I'll be tonight."

He pulled up to the shop and said, "Then get yo ass out my car and go turn up and make that money."

I laughed so hard I could barely open the door. It was always good times when he was around. He was nothing but jokes. After all that I had been through those past few days, it was nice to have a good laugh.

The Final Chapter: A New Beginning

I picked up my car and headed home, talking to myself the whole way there. Going over everything I needed to do and trying to figure out what I was going to wear tonight. All the kids were at their friends' houses and Deon was with Sheila, so that gave me a moment to myself at home.

It was different with the kids not being there, it was quiet; a small moment to sit and think about how blessed I'd been those past few months. It was hard sometimes when you had kids around, with the hustle and bustle of everything going on, to be able to have a mindful moment. I was running off of four hours of sleep today, but I was excited for tonight and wanted to find something cute to wear.

I started pulling everything out my closet and tried on at least eight outfits in the last hour. The very last one I pulled out, which was something Christian had gotten for me when we were in California, I decided that this one would be the one I would wear. I did think about him from time to time, but I couldn't really get involved with him. Trying to take care of the kids and Deon wouldn't have left any time or energy for him.

I decided to take a quick nap before I started to get ready. I set my alarm for five-thirty, giving myself enough time to get up, shower, dress, and do my makeup and to head over to the spot. The time must've flown by because I was up in no time. Normally, I would have put on some music while I got ready just to get myself amped up and ready for a video shoot, but tonight, I didn't; just took my time in the quiet and got myself ready. I slipped on my panties, put on my skirt and my top, unwrapped my hair and headed out the door. The GPS said it would take an hour to get to the location and I only had about forty-five minutes to get there. I was doing about 80 mph on the highway but texted Asia to let her know that I was on my way. Surely, she was busy getting ready herself and probably wouldn't even see my text, but I at least wanted to communicate with her to let her know I would be there as soon as I could.

The closer I got to the place, the more I wondered if I was even in the right area. I was on these back roads I had never been on before and ended up near these warehouses. I wasn't sure it was the right place.

I remembered she texted me her manager's number, so I called him. "Hey, I think I'm in the right place but where exactly do I go?"

"Oh yea, just pull up to the back building and come up to Suite 2."

"Okay cool; be up in a sec."

I found a spot to park, fixed my hair, pushed up my little itty-bitty titties, added some lip gloss, hopped out the car, and headed inside. The first person that I ran into introduced himself; it was her manager. He was fine as fuck. He gave me a hug with his big handsome self. I got a thing for big niggas and he was looking really good to me, but I wasn't there for that; I was there for her.

He said, "We'll be starting soon. You know black folks ain't never on time for nothing."

I laughed and said, "It's cool. I'm just happy to be here."

I went and sat down by the vending machine and called my girlfriend, CiCi. "Bitchhhhh, you need to be down her at this shoot tonight. Where you at?"

She replied, "I know, babe, but I've been so busy modeling my clothes and shoe line that I've been completely tied up lately."

We chatted for a little bit and even though she said she would try to make it there, by the time she arrived and got ready, we would be done.

The producer started calling for the models and dancers, so I told CiCi that I would talk to her about it another time. I went over to the set and stood there admiring how amazing it looked. Then I looked over and I saw Asia walk in looking beautiful. Her smile lit up the room and her energy was amazing. She saw me and motioned for me to come over and gave me a hug.

"Thank you for inviting me. This is so great."

"Oh, girl, please; it was no doubt that I wouldn't have you here. Enjoy yourself and have fun tonight, okay?"

I loved how loving and caring she was. She was so supportive, unlike some of my other friends. In the midst of cutting people off, Keyonna was cut off, too. She hadn't really been the same since we got back from Cali. She felt like she was better than me, but I chucked it up as her loss; not mine. I was for anyone that had a good heart and was willing to share success with others.

The studio was becoming more live and lit by the minute. People were coming in and out, the music was dope, and the models were all doing their thing. Asia came out and rocked her verses and put in work for about an hour straight. When she took her break, me and the other dancers and some of the models stepped in to shoot our scenes. Just being in that moment made me appreciate the sacrifices I'd made along the way. I was proud of myself for staying motivated and focused because if I wasn't, that moment right there, right then, wouldn't have happened.

Once it was all over, people were hanging out taking pics and vibing. A few celebrities had popped in and we were all standing around taking pics and having a good time.

I walked over to Asia. "Hey, boo! This was so great! Thanks so much for inviting me!"

She was super excited to see me. "Of course, girl! Once we wrap up here, I have a show tonight. You gonna come?"

"Of course, I am, I'm out here tonight, boo!"

She said, "Bet! Let me go put in these extra shots and then we can load up in the Sprinter and head out."

They had to redo a few shots, so I was off to the side recording her and taking a few pics so she could have them to post up for behind-the-scenes stuff. I took a few shots of

Henny to warm up before we hit the club. It was so much going on in that last twenty minutes, but it was so worth it all. Asia was done shooting and was ready to hit the club. Everyone hit the dressing rooms really quick to fix their makeup and change clothes. I was busy taking pics of everything and everyone to capture the moment. Watching Asia get ready for her show at the club was amazing to see. Knowing that one day, that would be me!

We arrived at the club on the Eastside of Atlanta, and everyone exited the Sprinter. We all flashed our IDs and headed inside. Her manager had hooked us up and we didn't have to pay anything. We were in there deep as hell in our own VIP section. Bottles coming to the table, shots being poured. It was nothing short of a celebration for her accomplishments and to our friendship; with a toast to myself as well. Everyone was dancing and singing; camera men were walking around filming the strippers and other dancers, too. It was just like the video shoot without actually being on set.

The DJ shouted out Asia, "Ayo, Asia, where you at, baby girl!"

She ran up to the stage, grabbed the mic, and once the DJ dropped her beat, the crowd went wild. Everyone in there was singing her words and rapping along with her. The song was a hit, and she smashed her performance. We all stuck around for about another thirty minutes after she performed and then all met up outside. Her manager had us all get back into the Sprinter to take us back to our cars. He wanted to make sure we all got home safely. I gave her and her manager a hug and thanked her for a wonderful night and wished her luck on everything. Told her I would see her around real soon.

On my way home, my phone was going off and because I was driving, I could only see the top portion of the notification and it said important message. Once I got to a red light, I opened it to see what it was. I tapped the link and couldn't believe what I was reading:

Alesha,

Congratulations on being our new cast member. You have been chosen to be a part of our new T.V. series and would like for you to be on set tomorrow at 3 p.m. sharp!

I couldn't even read the rest of the message. My hands were shaking, my heart was racing, and I didn't know whether I should scream or cry tears of joy. I could feel the adrenaline rushing through me and I was trying my best to contain it until I got home. I couldn't help but smile the rest of the way home. I was super excited because everything I went through led me to this moment and I couldn't be more grateful. I got home, showered and tried my best to get some sleep. I felt like I wanted to smoke but, instead, I floated on the cloud of good news until I passed out.

The next morning, I still wasn't sure if I wanted to share the good news or even who to share it with, but once I saw that the producers had shared my cover photo as one of the newest cast members, I decided to share it with the world and put it up all over my social media pages. I made sure to call and check in with the kids and checked in with Sheila to see how Deon was doing and they were all fine and doing well. I fixed myself some breakfast and started getting myself together for my big day on set. I got my things together and double-checked to make sure I wasn't forgetting anything. I had about an hour drive ahead of me and didn't want to have to turn back to get something I left behind.

By the time I made it there, I had to go straight to hair and makeup. Before turning my phone off, I got a call from Miss Angela. I wasn't sure if I wanted to answer, but I did.

"Hello."

"Hey, Alesha. I know we haven't spoken in a while, but I just wanted to say congratulations and that I'm proud of you."

"Thank you, Miss Angela, I appreciate that. I'm on set now so I can't talk. We'll catch up later."

"Okay, baby. Good luck today."

We said our goodbyes and hung up the phone. I saw a few other texts come through of congratulations and good luck, but I didn't have time to reply to anyone.

I was ready for set and as I stepped out there, I couldn't believe that I was really about to be doing what it was that I loved to do so much. I had never felt prouder of myself than that moment right there. I stayed true to what I believed in, stayed focused, stayed prayed up, and kept my faith in God that things would all work out in my favor when the time was right. I was a single mother but out living my dream. I dedicated myself to making changes and it had all paid off for me. I proved to myself that I could overcome any obstacle that came my way. It wasn't always easy, but I never stopped putting my best foot forward.

Once I wrapped for the day, I grabbed my things so that I could get ready to head home. I sat in the car and went through some of my messages, replying to some and ignoring others. However, there was one text from an unknown number that I read last.

Hey, this is Kenny. I hope all is well with you and my baby boy. I hope he's doing better, and I apologize to you and to him for the way I've treated you both these past couple years. It took me a while to realize how fucked up I was really mistreating you and to realize that I needed to be better and do better as a man. My son needs me and no matter what it is I have going on, I know I need to be there for him. I'm sorry.

I wasn't sure if I should even reply back. I wasn't sure if he was being sincere or if he was playing nice for the moment. I took a deep breath and decided to reply back:

Of course, he's fine, but I'm not going to try to pressure you anymore. I'm letting my foot up off ya neck and allowing you to be the one to make the decision as to whether you want to be involved or not. Trying to get everyone else to make you see how foul you were being wasn't doing anything but causing more problems and putting more stress on me. Deon is a great kid... will you ever make the time to come see him?

He is my son so, of course, I'm going to make the time to see him so that I can be a part of his life.

Well, I'll let you figure it out. I'm not going to force him on you. So, when you ready, you know how to reach me.

You can't ever force him on me. He's my son, so why would you say that?

I'm saying, if you would like to see him, that would be great. If not, that's okay, too. I would be willing to bring him to you or you can come to me, but the choice is ultimately up to you. I would love to be able to sit down and talk and try to come up with a plan for Deon. He really is the strongest and coolest kid, and you would love him if you gave it a chance. He looks just like you, too. All I ever wanted was for you to be there for him and help out when you can.

I waited for a reply and nothing. He vanished again as usual, or so I thought.

Alesha, I'm sorry, but I am ready to see him!"

I was shocked and grateful at the same time. I had so many thoughts going through my head at that moment, but I had to pull it together. Who would've thought that after months of calling, texting, blowing up his phone and trying to get everyone else to reach him, that all it took was for me to leave him alone for him to come around? I guess it was a brand-new day for everyone. I took this moment to just thank God for giving me the strength to not give up on myself. I landed the job I wanted, my kids were great, and I even had a brand-new beginning; hopefully for Deon and Kenny. There was nowhere else to go but up from there. I drove home that night thinking about what was next to come for me, for all of us because I was far from done. This was only just the beginning......

Made in the USA
Columbia, SC
20 July 2023

20670577R00086